About the Author

Linda Ward is a retired elementary school teacher who has been married to her husband and best friend since 1982.
They have three grown children, their spouses and five grandchildren. Her passion as a teacher was reading and teaching students to read.
Her first book, Jesus In The Manger, was published in 2017.
As a teacher in Texas, one of her favorite themes to teach was Texas history and explore the many environments, landscapes, wildlife and sheer vastness of the state. She moved from the deserts of West Texas to the North Texas area in 2019 to get closer to her children and grandchildren that live throughout Texas.
Linda's hobbies include Bible studies, cooking, gardening and being "Nana" to her precious grandkids and fur babies.

Linda Ward

I Spy
with my Boxer Eye

illustrated by László Veres & Penny Weber

I spy with my Boxer eyes,
Rocky Mountain ranges and desert basins,
Connected together under peaceful blue skies.
Delicate and exquisite are the scarce desert flowers;
The Yucca, the Barrel and Prickly Pear Cacti.

In my youthful romps in desert places
I chased rabbits, lizards, quail and doves.
Sometimes spring rains gave the perfect graces;
For the hidden poppies to magically appear
Creating a carpet of fanciful dancing yellow faces.

Careful observers can hear animal duets
Of coyotes and hawks in the cool desert nights.
While mountains change colors in majestic sunsets;
Brown, green and grey become orange, blue and purple
Creating a spectacular canvas one never forgets.

I spy with my Boxer eyes,
Palo Duro Canyon in the Texas Panhandle.
The landscape is changing where the Eastern sun rises;
Leaving canyons cut deep for great plains and tall grasses,
Where oil jacks and windmills display manmade devices.

Continuing South and some to the East,
Again the land changes into the Texas Hill Country.
Armadillos, raccoons and deer are just a few of the beasts;
Making homes in the Live Oak and Pecan trees protection,
Look closely for Bluejays and Cardinals, for a colorful feast.

Spring paints these Hills with Bluebonnets and Wildflowers,
While Mockingbirds sing songs they can mimic from others;
Like insects, amphibians and other birds, while singing for hours.
This is also the place where the Alamo still stands,
An unmistakable landmark against the sky where it towers.

I spy with my Boxer nose,

Distinctive smells of the Coastal Wetlands.

With beaches, tide pools and sand in my toes;

Returning back here to the place I was born

Where the sun rises early and the wind always blows.

The coastlines are rich with plants, animals and shells;
Where land meets the sea, white waves will greet you.
On beaches where Crabs, Pelicans and Seagulls dwell;
Sea Turtles will migrate to their breeding beds,
Laying eggs in the sand driven by instinct and smells.

A fisherman's paradise is this salty sea air;
Playful Dolphins ride waves and Sharks sneak about,
Making fish stories more interesting for all those who share.
Hours of sunlight, endless beaches with friends
The largest Gulf playground just about anywhere.

I spy with my Boxer ears,

From the Coast going North to Blackland Prairies and Lakes

I now roam through rich woodlands, it gives me such cheers.

Growing up in the desert, I thought that was hot;

But these lakes, rivers, streams provide humidity that seers.

In my North Texas home my senses have found
Squirrels chirping and taunting me and rabbits make chases,
Where Pecan, Oak and Maple trees cover the ground.
Crape Myrtles bloom everywhere and so do the flowers.
God's spectacular gardens make me one happy hound.

Texas regions are vast and I did my best,
To share landscapes and regions of this magnificent state.
Truly there's no place quite like it from the East to the West.
Go explore if you will Mountains, Lakes, Prairies and Plains
The Hill Country, Woodlands, and Gulf Coast, you will surely be blessed!

About the Illustrators

Laszlo Veres has been a professional illustrator for 30 years.
He uses computer technology, mainly various 3D software applications,
to make his very detailed, life-like illustrations.
He resides in Hungary.

Penny Weber is an illustrator from Long Island, New York.
She draws and paints her pictures digitally using Adobe Photoshop.
Penny lives with her husband, three children
and their very fat cat Tiger.

www.ingramcontent.com/pod-product-compliance
Lightning Source LLC
Chambersburg PA
CBRC090735150426
42811CB00067B/1916